An Introduction to African Wildlife for Kids

Amazing Animal Books for Young Readers

Muhammad Usman

Mendon Cottage Books

JD-Biz Publishing

Our books are available at

1. Amazon.com
2. Barnes and Noble
3. Itunes
4. Kobo
5. Smashwords
6. Google Play Books

Download Free Books!

http://MendonCottageBooks.com

Table of Contents

Introduction

I want to thank you for downloading the book, "An Introduction to the African Wildlife for Kids"

This book is a realistic guide that will teach your kids about the wonderful animals that exist on the continent of Africa. For the purpose of conserving the diversity of life, it is important to consider, that every single animal mentioned in this book deserves a lot of care and that anyone can take the necessary steps to make sure that they continue to exist. A big part of the book covers the history of these animals, where they are usually found, what they eat, and that sort of thing; there's a lot to be learnt from this book, but if you just want to jump right in and look at the lovely animals, so that you are aware of them, the pictures will suffice.

It is the hope of the author that you'll actually get to learn more about these remarkable African animals so that you can appreciate them and maybe even visit the continent of Africa to see how they look like in their natural habitat. This book talks more about the treasures of African wildlife; a sneak-peek into the life of spectacular wild animals found in the Mother-Continent. Enjoy!

AFRICAN WILDCATS

African has a vast number of cat's species that occupy different habitats from the savanna to the dense forests. These cats vary in size and adaptation to the eco system. The largest cat in Africa is the lion followed by the leopard. Other smaller cats that exist include the serval. Here is a look at some big cats in Africa and several small once.

Africa's Big Cats

Lions

This is a cat that you will find in almost all parts of Africa; from the Northern sub-Saharan deserts to the southern parts of Africa. It is also the second largest cat in the wild. This cat hardly lives more than ten to fourteen years in the wild. This is because of injuries sustained from continual fighting with other rival males; hence reducing their longevity. Lions in captivity, however, can live for more than twenty years. Lions in Africa are known to occupy Savannah and grassland territories but may also be found in the bushes and forests. This cat is a social cat compared to other cats that have a solitary life; they live in groups called pride which is lead by a single dominant male and a group of females. The hunting is done by females of the pride while the male plays a protective role. The male lion is larger than the female with prominent mane which grows downwards and backward. The mane may cover the head and neck area.

Leopards

This cat is the second largest cat in Africa. It is very elusive and difficult to spot. It is considered to be very beautiful since its short fur has large spots that are arranged in rosettes. This cat has a robust build and is well adapted to different habitats. The leopard is known for its stealth, especially when stalking prey. Leopards are known nocturnal, and are therefore active at night; this cat has the ability to climb and can be seen resting on tree branches during the day to avoid the hot sun or at times dragging their kill up the trees, away from the hyenas reach. The leopard is a very agile animal.

The Cheetah

The cheetah is a slender cat with spots on its coat and has black flash-like streaks on its face. It also has long thin but very powerful legs that are specially modified for high speed. This cat is active mainly during the day when its biggest activity is hunting. It is renowned all over the world given that it is the fastest land mammal and can reach speeds of up to one hundred and twenty-kilo meter per hour when hunting. There most preferred prey is the Thomson's gazelle. Cheetahs are mostly confused to leopards because of the spots but the distinction is in size

Africa's Small Cats

Africa has several small cats that occupy the continent and hunt game on their own right. These small cats are mostly over looked because most of the attention is given to the big cats; this is because of their conservation status. A good example of some of these cats are as follows.

Caracal

This is a medium sized cat that has very beautiful ears with elongated hair sticking on the tip of the ears called tufts. This hair is said to also play in trapping sound vibrations. It has a robust body and the coat is reddish or sandy in color. The caracal is nocturnal meaning it is most active during the night. It is best known for its areal acrobats when catching birds. It is an expert bird catcher and makes up ninety percent of its diet. The caracal is often confused with the lynx another small cat because both have tufted ears, but it is easy to tell the difference since the lynx is spotted. Because of its small build, this cat can climb very well and ambush birds while waiting in tree branches.

Caracal

Serval

The serval is known for its huge ears that are well adapted to listening. This cat is famous because it is able to catch prey without even seeing it. It uses its large cup like ears to listen even under the ground and pounce on its prey with huge areal lips surprising the animal. The serval's coat is golden yellow and extensive spots and stripes run on the body. It is a slender medium sized cat that is famous for standing still for hours listening to the ground using its large ears for rodents moving underground and lips in the air and drop once on top of its prey item.

A mother serval with her baby

BIRDS OF AFRICA

The African continent is diverse in its ecosystem which supports a large number of very beautiful birds that are both large and small. These birds are known to be flightless and others can fly. Birds on the African continent inhabit the forests, wetlands and the desert. Some lay their eggs in nests built on trees and some lay their eggs on the ground. One bird that is found almost everywhere on the African continent is the Common Ostrich. Let's have a look at some of the birds that are found on this continent.

Common Ostrich

This bird is a flight less bird known for its dance during the mating season. Another notorious attribute of the ostrich is its protective nature; ostriches habitually lay their eggs on the ground, this makes their eggs to become vulnerable prey for many animals, including humans. The male bird which is usually distinguished by its darker color is the one that cares for the eggs; strange! This behavior is in contrast to that of other birds in general. For most birds, it is the female that does the work of sitting on the eggs until they hatch, but this is not so for the flighty ostrich.

And just because an ostrich does not fly, does not mean that this bird is slow. It is arguably the fastest bird on two feet and can reach speeds of up to seventy kilometers per hour; it is aided by its huge wings which trap air and act as stabilizers like on airplanes. This has an effect of reducing its weight making the bird fill light hence its speed. It is ranked the fastest animal on two feet. The ostrich is also known to soak its feathers in water from the nearest water source and rush to dampen its eggs during bush fires since the eggs are on the ground. This common ostrich is also notorious for laying its head and neck flat on the ground, forming a mold-like resemblance of earth from a distance.

Grey Crowned Crane

The gray crowned crane is another famous bird in Africa which is the national symbol for the Ugandan nation and also known as the Ugandan crane. The crowned crane mostly walks in pairs a male and a female. The crane can reach up to a meter in height and weight to three kilograms. The crowned crane has a wing span of two meters and it gets its name from a crown of stiff golden feathers on the head.

Grey Crowned Crane

Lesser Flamingo

The flamingo is a well-known bird in Africa. Mostly found on shores of sodic lakes of the African continent. This bird has a pink coloration that it gets from feeding on shrimps. The darker the pink color the older the bird. The flamingo is known to migrate from Eastern Africa to Europe following the seasons. The flamingo has large populations in Lake Nakuru and Lake Bogoria both in Kenya. This bird has a primary breeding site at Lake Natron and only migrates to Europe for feeding during the summer. They are very powerful flying birds and can elevate themselves to high altitudes to catch winds that are traveling in a given direction to aid in migration. They find their way using magnetic location hence can fly through bad weather without getting lost. Flamingos are one of the protected birds since their population and habitat is being destroyed by human pollution and encroachment.

Flamingo

THE CONTINENT OF THE APES

The wonderful African continent has a wide range of small and great apes that are known to inhabit the dense tropical and equatorial forests. These apes find home and food in dense jungles of the continent. Primates are known to be very intelligent especially in adaptation to their environment. Most of the apes have complex behaviors that make them unique and different from each other, these behaviors include tool use and communication together with vocalization. Primates can be differentiated into two the great apes and small primates.

Africa's Small Primates

Monkeys

Monkeys are very cunning and clever, they are known to observe and understand their environment and adapt to it. Because of their size which is small monkeys are very agile on trees and spend most of their time on them feeding and staying out of reach from predators. Here are some common African monkeys you may want to know.

Colobus Monkey

It is the white and black colobus monkey which has thick fur that is beautiful with black and white patches. The colobus monkey feeds on fruit and leaves and lives in large groups called troops. Members of the troop are known to care for new born babies that are left by their mothers. The colobus monkey also plays an important role in the dispersal of seeds in the forest because they feed on fruits and drop the seeds on the ground allowing new trees to grow. Some African communities are known to eat colobus monkeys as bush meat.

A red colobus monkey

Sykes Monkey

This monkey is a small monkey that has smooth short fur and a long tail. It is also known as the white throat monkey because of the white coloration around the throat area. This monkey has eye brows that are bushy and protruding making the face look curious. They are known to be very invasive in people's plantations and have to be chased out of farms.

Sykes Monkey eating fruit in the trees

The Vervet Monkey

Vervet Monkey in a tree

This monkey has a black face with a white fringe of hair on the eyebrows. It is famous for its playful nature and canning ability. They also take a lot of time to care for each other which is known as grooming. This helps them remove parasites from their bodies and aid in bonding with each other. Their long tail has a function of adding balance when moving in the tree canopy. In some areas, they are known to be friendly to humans because of periodic feeding.

Baboon

The baboon is a primate that lives on the ground in the African savannah. Their face has a dog-like muzzle with a sharp canine. The female carries the babies on the back and at times on the under belly when running. The baboon is also known to be very aggressive and hunts vervet monkeys and small antelope. Because of their aggressive nature, they at times raid human dwelling and prey on sheep and goat.

The Great Apes of Africa

These are big primates of Africa which include the Gorilla and Chimpanzee. Most of the great apes in Africa are found in the equatorial region because of the dense jungle environment in this area.

The Gorilla

Silverback Gorilla

When you hear about the gorilla what comes to mind is the famous Godzilla or the chest beating that is known to be a territorial display of the male gorilla. This primate has no tail but displays a high level of agility in the trees. The gorilla can walk upright for short distances and is also know to use tools. The use of tools by great apes shows that they are very intelligent. The gorilla is known to use a stick to test the depth of standing water pools to estimate depth since it cannot swim. This primate is also very aggressive and will attack people if it feels threatened.

Chimpanzee

A mother chimpanzee holding her cub on a mangrove tree branch

The chimpanzee is a much smaller ape compared to the gorilla but is the world's most intelligent ape that has been known to be trained even to drive a car. This primate can use a wide variety of tools in the wild even stones to open nuts, sticks to remove ants from holes and observe human behavior and imitate what they are doing. It is said when given time chimpanzee can solve a majority of problems. When you talk about a chimpanzee what comes to mind is tool use. They are known to modify sticks and sharpen them with stones to perform a specific function.

Majority of wild life in Africa comprises of large animals that feed on plants. These are hoofed animals which occupy the savannas and forests. They are an important aspect of wild life since they are the prey that supports the predator population

AFRICA'S FAVORITE HERBIVORES

Africa has a large number of herbivores these are animals that feed on plant material alone. These animals range in size from small to big animals and make up a large number of the animals found on this continent. Some of these animals also provide game meat for the local communities in Africa.

Elephant

African Elephant

This is the largest land mammal and is famous for their ivories which are actually teeth. The elephant is an iconic animal because it has a life span almost as that of humans. One feature that makes the elephant well known is that it has a good memory and would visit places that it visited a long time ago. Elephants, despite their large size, are very good swimmers and can swim for kilometers. The elephant also uses their feet to listen, they can detect ultra sonic waves through their feet and communicate this way using low-frequency rambles. Despite them having eyes they have a poor eye sight and can only see up to up to a meter away and rely on a keen sense of smell to detect their environment. The big ears have another role apart from listening; they act as a ventilation system that helps cool the body and regulate temperature.

Giraffe

Giraffe are the tallest land living mammal in the World, ranging from 16 - 18 feet tall. They live mostly in the sub-Saharan savanna areas of Africa. Their extremely long neck and tongue help them eat leaves from the tallest trees; they really like acacia trees. They sleep less than 2 hours per day; most of the time they are eating, they eat about 100 pounds of leaves and twigs everyday!

Giraffe babies take 15 months to grow in their mother's belly, and then the mother gives birth while standing up! The baby can stand within 15 minutes of being born; they are on average about 6 feet tall at birth.

Most giraffes live about 25 years in the wild.

A mother giraffe with her baby

Cape Buffalo

When one hears about the Cape buffalo what comes to mind aggressive nature of this animal and is responsible for the majority of the human wildlife deaths that occur in Africa. Some communities in Africa call it the Black Death because it has a black coat and often attacks humans. The Cape buffalo is known to stand its ground when attacked by lions and at times kills lions. It has very large horns that curve upwards which it uses to protect its self. The Buffalo can also swim and is known to run in neck deep waters when it fills threatened or attacked by lions.

Wildebeest

The wildebeest moved into the genes books of record as a wonder of the world because of its migration from the Tanzanian Serengeti national park through the crocodile infested Mara River to the Masai Mara national reserve. The wildebeest can give birth while moving and the calf is ready to walk and run with the herd in less than fifteen minutes. It is an iconic animal in the African continent because of its long migration that occurs in the months of June and July.

Migrating wildebeest

Kudu

This is an important antelope for the African continent since time in memorial most indigenous communities value the horn of this antelope and use it as a musical instrument. The Kudu has a long horn that twists upward and a hole is made at the top near the tip of the horn at a specific angle and when the air is blown in the horn it produces a low-frequency bass note. This is used in traditional or folk songs. The antelope is identified by its distinctive horns and white streaks on its face appearing as tears flowing from the eyes. This is a big antelope and is very territorial.

Kudu

Oryx

The Oryx is an arid dwelling antelope that is famous for its very long horns up to a meter and a half that face slightly backward but are almost upright. The horns are not very large in diameter as compared to the kudu and have screw-like threads that twist along the length of the horn. Despite being not very large the Oryx has few predators' cats because it has the ability to fend off any big cat that tries to attack from the back since its long horns are able to stab ant predator that tries to jump on its back. It also can run very fast up to fifty kilometers per hour and go without water for weeks. It can survive on moister it obtains from the plants it eats.

Eland

The Eland is a very big antelope and it's known for its sweet tasting meat. It is one of the most preferred game meat antelopes in Africa. A mature eland can weigh up to two hundred kilograms. Because of its commercial nature, their numbers are small in the wild and are being protected by most countries in Africa.

Thomson's Gazelle

This is a small animal almost the size of a domestic goat. It gets its reputation as one of the fastest gazelles and is the favored prey item for the cheetah. This gazelle can reach speeds of ninety kilometers per hour. It is very swift and agile to escape from predators.

Dik Dik

It is one of the smallest antelope species and might weigh only ten kilograms. Local African myths say that this antelope is fast to the extent it starts bush fires by the friction it generates from running on dry grass.

Dik Dik antelope eating an acacia tree

THE REPTILES OF AFRICA

Africa has a wide range of reptiles ranging from lizards to snakes which survive in different habitats on the continent. The African reptiles are very tolerant of the harsh climate found on the continent.

Monitor lizard

The monitor lizard is a lizard famed for its powerful tail which it uses to defend its self from predators and fight with each other. This tail is so powerful that it can whip a human's leg off. The monitor lizard has a tough scaly skin which protects the animal. It also has long curved claws and a split tongue that it uses to smell the environment. This lizard is notorious in Africa for stealing eggs which are a favorite, hence coming into contact with humans on their farms. The monitor lizard can be said to be semi aquatic because it prefers wetlands or coastal regions. It is a powerful swimmer and uses its powerful tail to swim. Most communities in Africa use the monitor lizards skin to make drums because it is tough and would not tear even when over stretched. The lizard lays its eggs on the sandy banks of rivers, lakes or beaches and the female might protect them from other male lizards until they hatch. The young ones live on tree branches because they can be preyed on. They will stay up the trees until they are big enough to walk on land.

Black Mamba

This snake can be said to be an important snake of the African continent with more deaths recorded under it than any known African snake. It is also the longest venomous snake in Africa with a length of over four meters. The black mamba is known to chase humans when provoked and can travel up to sixteen kilometers per hour or six point eight meters per second. The black mamba also is the fastest moving snake indigenous to Africa. Another important fact is that the black mamba can raise sixty percent of its body from the ground especially when provoked. In Africa, a bite from the black mamba was almost 100% fatal until 1996 when an antivenom was developed.

Eastern Green Mamba

When one hears of the green mamba you think of the lash coastal tropical forests of Africa which provide a camouflage for this snake. It is a long snake that can reach three meters in length. This snake venom is very toxic containing toxins that attack the nerves and heart. It lives mostly on trees and hardly moves on the ground. The green mamba has a green coat and a yellowish under belly.

Cape Cobra

This snake is yellow in some geographical areas or brown in color. The cape cobra produces a hood when provoked and its venom is very poisonous with neurotoxic components. This snake is found in arid areas of Africa mostly the southern parts of the continent.

A baby Cape Cobra

African Rock Python

When you hear of the African rock python what one thinks is the powerful nature of this snake known to bring down large prey the size of a single cow. The python is known to kill its prey with constriction. It squeezes its prey any time it exhales until the animal suffocates. The rock python is the largest snake in Africa and is not venomous. This snake is ranked the sixth largest snake in the world.

WEIRD ANIMALS LIVING IN AFRICA

Aardvark

This weird nocturnal usually eats termites and ants. The Aardvark has a very good sense of smell and it uses this to find food. Whenever this animal sees its prey, it uses its long, sticky tongue to capture its prey.

Known for its expertise in digging, the aardvark normally burrows its way out of danger whenever there's a predator nearby.

Although they are sometimes mistaken for pigs, since they look so much alike, the aardvark is the only remaining species of the order Tubulidentata.

Aardwolf

This is one weird nocturnal creature whose name literally means 'earth wolf.' These animals can be found in the eastern and southern scrublands of Africa. The Aardwolf is closely related to the hyena; however, an interesting fact about it is that it doesn't feed on meat; just insects, and especially termites. Yummy! Did you know that this bizarre looking can capture and eat up to 250,000 termites in one night!

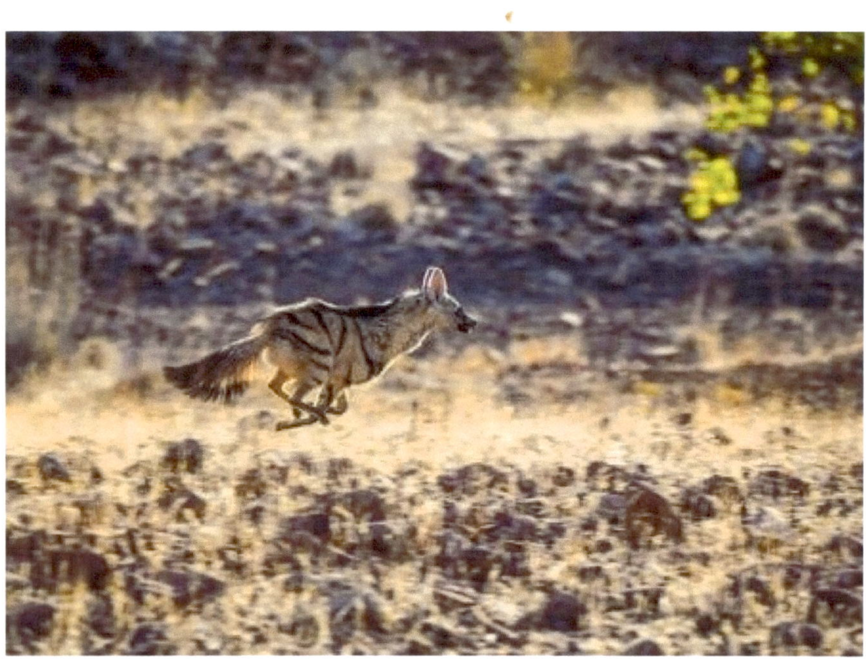

Guereza colobus monkeys (Colobus guereza)

This is one of the colobus monkey species that live in Africa. They can grow up to 5ft, with their tail taking over half its size. Like other monkeys, they like to live in closed forests. An interesting fact about the Colobus guereza is that they rarely come down from the trees. They have an interesting jumping technique that allows them to jump as high as 15m in the air as they travel from branch to branch; they are able to do this by using their long tail to keep balance and the hair on their shoulders act as a parachute, reducing their momentum as they land on a branch.

Okapi

The ever shy, rarely-seen Okapi lives in the jungle forests of central Africa. They are closely related to the giraffes even though they look like zebras; the weird markings on the hide provide camouflage in the forest environment.

Okapi

Pangolin

Pangolin

Whenever the pangolin is sighted, one cannot avoid noticing its distinctive thick, armor-like coat. Scientists claim that this coat is made out of a material known as keratin; the same type of material that is found in hair and fingernails.

The Pangolin is also nocturnal and it lives in tree hollows or in burrows. They like to eat termites and ants.

African civet

The African civet can grow up to 84cm in length, with an extra 47cm for its tail. They can weigh anywhere between 9kg up to 20kg. To see the African Civet in its natural habitat is not that difficult as it can be found in the African highlands, lowlands, swamps, forests, and even in the open savannah, where there's long grass or enough thickets for shelter. They also have a very broad diet that includes small mammals, crabs, and millipedes; their diet changes with the habitat they are in. Different African civets are known to have different coat patterns, consisting of black and brown spots. This color blend on their coats provides excellent camouflage in their habitat.

Did you know that the African civet has the ability to produce a secretion that was once used as a very important ingredient in perfumes?

Lemur

Many people in the world have never had the chance to see this primate; most people don't even know whether they exist. But thanks to the movie "Madagascar," these primates have become very famous. Like most primates living in the African jungles, the Lemur in the movie is a self-proclaimed king, which says a lot about its character.

That being said, did you know that evolution experts claim that the lemur was once as large as an adult gorilla?! Imagine how it looked like back then. It is believed that the reason why they got smaller was in order to adapt to living in trees and also to survive on less food.

A mother ring-tailed lemur and her babies

Springhare

You've got to agree that this is one of the strangest hare-like specimens, you've ever seen. This exclusively nocturnal vegetarian is an "evolved" hare species with kangaroo-like hind legs! The Springhare likes to live in burrows in sandy soils. They also like to live in pairs, and whenever you see them you'll notice that they are usually just part of larger springhare communities.

The best place one can spot this strange looking "bunny" would be in East Africa. Perhaps, if you ever get the chance to visit Tanzania's Ngorongoro Conservancy, you are more than likely to see them at night, if you will be staying at Ndutu Lodge.

An interesting thing about these nocturnal hares is that they have bright shiny eyes, which can be easily spotted using a flashlight at night; therefore, you can easily search for them!

Elephant Shrew

As we conclude the list of weird African animals, we cannot forget to discuss the Elephant shrew's imposing snout. This little mouse-like insectivore is quite rare and has a rather strange but beautiful coat. They are distributed across different biomes of Southern Africa. Currently, there are over 10 species of elephant shrews widespread across the continent of Africa.

Elephant Shrews are very funny creatures; you'll definitely love to watch them in their habitat. They usually sniff out small invertebrates from the ground, and collect them using their tongues!

Conclusion

It is the hope of the author that book was able to enlighten you concerning the most cherished animals from the continent of Africa. Children who love life and the enjoy the aspect of learning more about animals in the wild will really enjoy this book and will probably learn more about what Africa's wildlife has to offer.

Fancy a trip to Africa to actually see these animals in their natural habitat?

Author Bio

Dr. Muhammad Usman. MD, B.Sc.

Dr. Muhammad Usman a medical graduate from Allama Iqbal Medical Collagen (AIIMC). He is currently undertaking his specialist physician training in internal medicine. He is a certified nutritionist has a B.Sc. degree in nutrition with majors in micro-nutrition. He is a prolific researcher and serving as an editor in a number of peer-reviewed research journals.

In the last 5 years, Dr. Usman has helped countless people achieve their health, fitness, and weight loss goals through his writings, training, and coaching sessions.

His other experiences include working as an independent researcher. He has got more than 25 publications in peer-reviewed medical journals on topics related to endocrinology, internal medicine, psychiatry, surgery, pulmonology, ophthalmology, and nephrology. He is a passionate writer and has produced thousands of blog posts, detailed guides, and books on topics related to health, fitness, and nutrition.

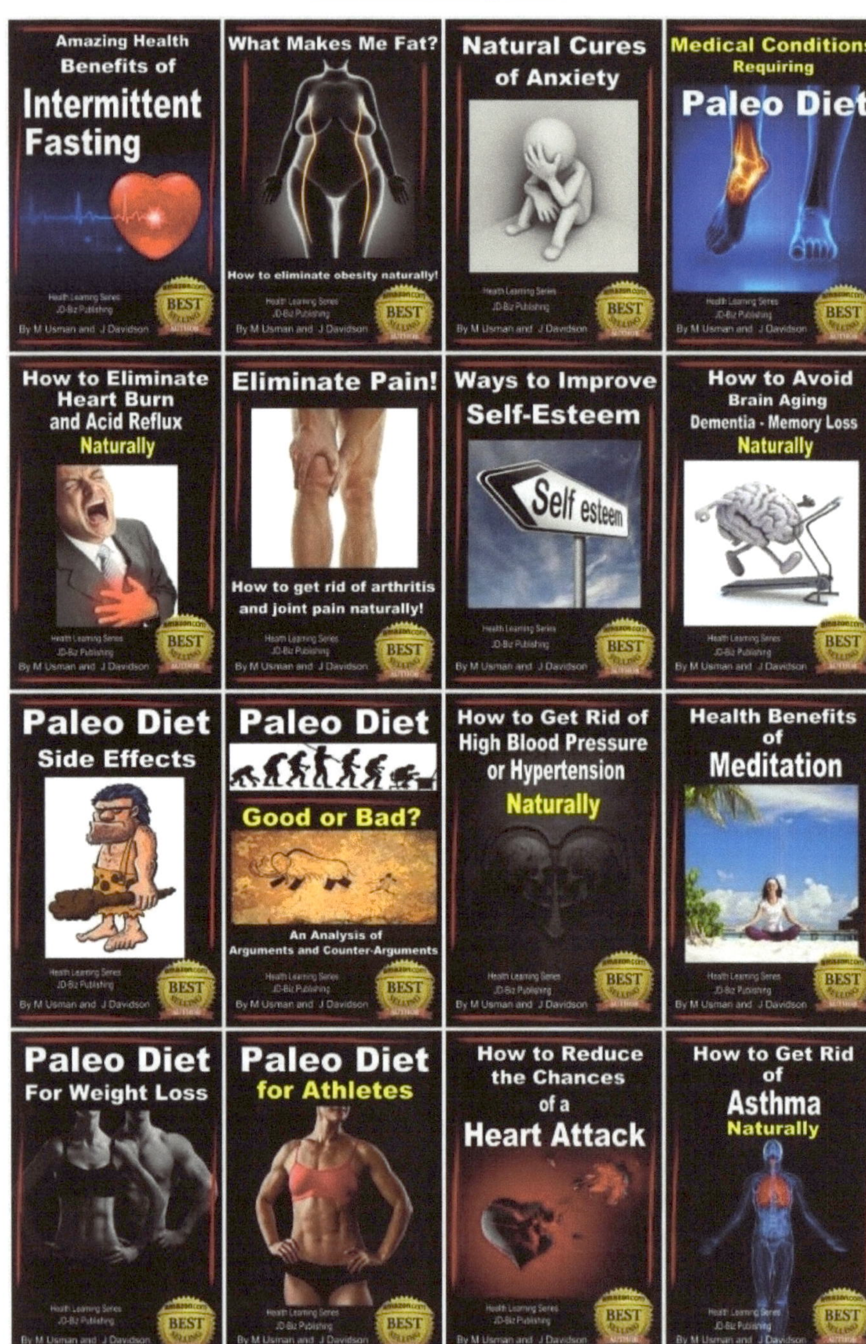
Amazing Health Benefits of Intermittent Fasting
What Makes Me Fat?
How to eliminate obesity naturally!
Natural Cures of Anxiety
Medical Conditions Requiring Paleo Diet
How to Eliminate Heart Burn and Acid Reflux Naturally
Eliminate Pain!
How to get rid of arthritis and joint pain naturally!
Ways to Improve Self-Esteem
How to Avoid Brain Aging Dementia - Memory Loss Naturally
Paleo Diet Side Effects
Paleo Diet Good or Bad?
An Analysis of Arguments and Counter-Arguments
How to Get Rid of High Blood Pressure or Hypertension Naturally
Health Benefits of Meditation
Paleo Diet For Weight Loss
Paleo Diet for Athletes
How to Reduce the Chances of a Heart Attack
How to Get Rid of Asthma Naturally

Our books are available at

1. Amazon.com

2. Barnes and Noble

3. Itunes

4. Kobo

5. Smashwords

6. Google Play Books

Download Free Books!

http://MendonCottageBooks.com

Publisher

JD-Biz Corp

P O Box 374

Mendon, Utah 84325

http://www.jd-biz.com/